Ancient India

Rosie McCormick

Core Knowledge

ISBN: 978-1-68380-436-9

Ancient India

Table of Contents

Chapter 1   **Mystery of the Indus** 2

Chapter 2   **Hinduism** 5

Chapter 3   **Festival of Lights** 9

Chapter 4   **The Story of the Buddha** 12

Chapter 5   **A Jataka Tale** 15

Chapter 6   **King Asoka** 17

Mystery of the Indus

A long time ago, the Indus people lived in a river valley south of the great mountains in India. These mountains are the Himalayas, the highest mountains

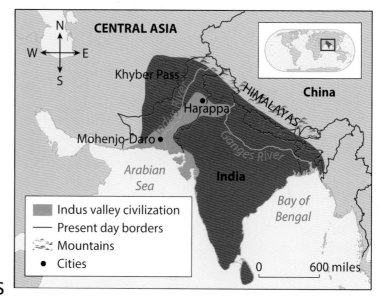

in the world. This Indus valley civilization developed at about the same time as ancient Mesopotamia and ancient Egypt.

The Indus River valley civilization grew strong thanks to the Indus River. Whenever the Indus River flooded, rich soil was carried onto the farmland by the overflowing waters. The rich soil helped food crops grow. More crops meant that more people could be fed.

We know that the Indus people had a written language made up of symbols. But we do not know what all the symbols mean.

The Indus valley civilization is still a mystery. There is much we do not understand. We do know that the Indus people built large cities that were home to thousands of people. One of these ancient cities was called Mohenjo-Daro (/mo*hen*joh/ dah*roh/). It had brick buildings and streets that were neatly laid out in straight lines.

Many artifacts, or objects, that once belonged to the Indus people have been found in the ruins of the ancient cities. Because of these findings, we know that the Indus people made beautiful gold and silver jewelry.

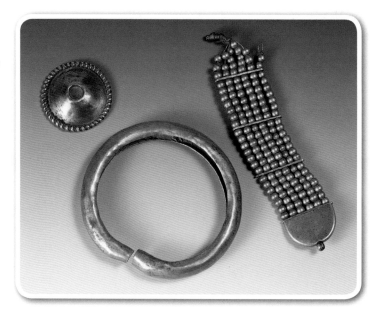

We know that they made tiny statues of animals and people and that the bull was an important symbol. But why was the bull so important? We can guess, but we cannot say for sure!

Hinduism

More than three thousand years ago, Aryan invaders came to the Indus River area. They did not farm. Instead they moved from place to place with their herds of animals.

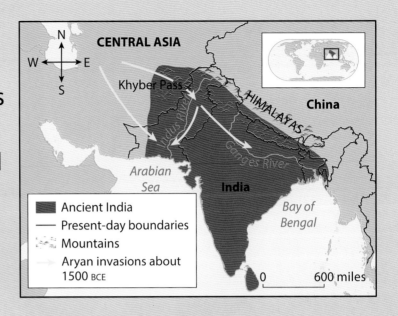

The Aryans captured and burned many Indus cities. They moved across India and eventually gained control of large areas. The Aryan people used war chariots pulled by horses in battle.

The Aryans brought their beliefs about how the world started and how people should live to India. Over time, their beliefs and those of the Indus people were woven together. As a result, a new religion called Hinduism became the main religion in India.

The Hindu religion has several holy books. The most important books are called Vedas. *Veda* means knowledge.

The oldest holy book is the Rig Veda. It is more than three thousand years old. The Rig Veda contains stories and songs that come from the Aryans. The Rig Veda has stories of Agni. Agni is the Hindu god of fire. It is Agni, Hindus say, who keeps their homes warm and cozy in winter and cooks their dinners.

Hindus believe that Brahma created the world. With four faces, he can look east, west, north, and south at the same time.

Shiva is the Hindu god of destruction. The third eye on his forehead lets him see what others can't. Shiva destroys and changes things. Vishnu is the god who protects the world. Vishnu is called the Preserver.

Hinduism is not just a religion. It is a way of life. It guides what Hindus eat, wear, and do in life. Since ancient times, Hindus have divided themselves into different groups, or castes.

A priest

A king

A military leader

A trader

A shopkeeper

A farmer

A craftsman

An outcaste

In ancient times, the most important caste was that of the priests. The second-highest caste was made up of military leaders and royal rulers, such as kings.

Festival of Lights

Diwali is the Hindu festival of lights. It is celebrated each year in October or November. The goddess Lakshmi is honored during this festival. She is the goddess of wealth and good luck. Because it is believed that Lakshmi likes everything to be clean and tidy, people get ready for Diwali by cleaning their homes.

During Diwali, clay containers, or bowls, filled with oil and a wick are lit.

People place the carefully prepared bowls on the Ganges River. They hope that Lakshmi will see the twinkling lights as they float along and grant them good luck!

Golden marigolds are added to the tiny bowls. The bowls are often made by hand.

Families buy new clothes for Diwali. Women in India wear saris. Saris look like long dresses, but they are actually made from one long piece of cloth. Saris are worn by wrapping the long piece of cloth around the waist to make a skirt. Then the end of the cloth is draped over the shoulder.

During Diwali, people go to the temples to pray. They bring gifts of food and flowers to Lakshmi and other Hindu gods and goddesses.

The Story of the Buddha

Long ago, in India, a royal baby was born. His name was Prince Siddhartha. His parents, the king and queen, were very happy. According to the legend, on the day he was born, Siddhartha was able to walk and talk.

The king ordered that the prince be given everything that would make him happy. He was not allowed to see anything that would make him sad. And he was not allowed to leave the royal palace.

And so Prince Siddhartha grew up not knowing about sickness and suffering. Then one day he left his royal home. What he saw outside the walls of the royal palace made him very sad. He saw people who were hungry and sick.

Prince Siddhartha wanted to stop such suffering. He set off on a journey in search of happiness and peace for all people. For a while he ate very little. He grew thin and unhealthy until he realized that if he was going to be helpful, he must be strong.

One day Siddhartha remembered that when he was a child he got his best ideas in the shade of a big, old tree. So he searched for a special tree—a Tree of Wisdom. Eventually Siddhartha found the Tree of Wisdom. For many, many days he sat beneath its beautiful branches and thought long and hard.

As a result of his deep thinking, Siddhartha found wisdom and knowledge. He found a perfect peace and love for all living things. He believed the wisdom he had gained would help everyone. Siddhartha became known as the Buddha, "the Enlightened One." For the rest of his life, he traveled and taught many people.

A Jataka Tale

The Buddha was a great teacher, and like many teachers, he told stories that taught a lesson. One of the Buddha's stories is about a frightened rabbit. The rabbit was frightened because one day, in a beautiful forest, the little rabbit suddenly heard a loud noise. "Help! The earth is breaking apart," yelled the rabbit as it hopped away as fast as it could.

Other animals heard the cries of the frightened rabbit, and they began to run too! Water buffalo ran. Tigers and wild pigs ran. Elephants ran. Soon, every animal in the forest was running.

Meanwhile, a lion was taking a nap on a cliff top. The thundering hooves of the animals woke the lion. The lion stepped out and stopped the animals before they fell off the cliff.

"Why are you running?" he roared.

"The earth is breaking apart," they cried.

"Have you seen it breaking apart?" the lion asked.

"Well, no! But the rabbit told us," the animals explained.

"Hmmmm!" said the lion. "Let us investigate."

And so they all set off to the place where the rabbit had first heard the noise. It was there they discovered that what the rabbit had heard was a coconut falling to the ground.

"This is a good lesson," said the lion. "It's important to know the facts before you act!" And all the animals agreed!

King Asoka

Long ago, in ancient India, there was a powerful king. His name was King Asoka. King Asoka won many battles and created a great empire. Then one day as King Asoka looked out over the land he had conquered, he realized that as well as achieving victory, he had caused great destruction. This made him sad.

Some time later, King Asoka came upon a poor man begging for food. The poor man stared at the king. It was not wise to stare at a king. King Asoka became curious. He wanted to meet the man who was clearly not afraid of him.

The king sat down next to the man, and they talked. The poor man was a holy man—a Buddhist monk. As they talked, the monk told the king how he could become a better ruler. He told King Asoka that he could use his power and wealth to help people.

From that day on, King Asoka lived a better life. He cared for people and animals. He built hospitals and roads. He provided wells so that people would have fresh water to drink.

The king became a Buddhist and spread the Buddha's teachings. In India, the lion became a symbol, or sign, of King Asoka's great power and good deeds.

Core Knowledge®

CKHG™

Core Knowledge HISTORY AND GEOGRAPHY™

Series Editor-in-Chief

E. D. Hirsch Jr.

Editorial Directors

Linda Bevilacqua and Rosie McCormick

Subject Matter Expert

Spencer Leonard, PhD